The Great Mother
and Other Poems

The Great Mother and Other Poems

Michele Murray

Sheed and Ward, Inc.
Subsidiary of Universal Press Syndicate
New York

Some of these poems have appeared in the following journals:
*Hanging Loose; Gnosis; Southern Poetry Review; Lace Review;
New; Nation; Apple; Pyramid; Woodwind; Dacotah Territory;
Earth's Daughters; Spectrum.* "The Woman Who Lives Inside the
World" was published in *A House of Good Proportion: Images
of Women in Literature* (Simon & Schuster).

The Great Mother and Other Poems

For further information address Sheed and Ward, Inc.
Subsidiary of Universal Press Syndicate,
475 Fifth Avenue, New York, New York 10017

ISBN-0-8362-0591-X
Library of Congress Card No. 74-9208.
Designed by Susan Thornton

To my husband

"to speak plainly . . .
comes hard. . ."

Contents

One

Two

Three

Four

Five

Six

One

Matins

Morning opens in the household of my body.
Brushing my hair I bend to the floor.
Loose hair falls down before me   crackling
away from the arc of my body.
Reflected in the tile   west-moving sun
alights on the trees outside
            on the skin of myself within:
consciousness rises in the body!

Broken shadows drift along the tiles;
lines the sun brushes: curve of thigh,
breasts swinging as I turn & raise my arms
to gather & to knot abounding hair.
No mirrors in this bone-stripped room.
I work by memory and gesture, catching
my body as it slides in & out of
overlapping light
                feeling it appear
to me again slowly after the absences
                of night;
new to my touch, a quickening body
disguised in wrinkles of time, imperfections
that the sun teases as this body which carries me
absorbs blue wakening   goes on   into
the ellipses of the day   companioned
stepping into the pathway of the sun
bodying forth myself in this risen hour.

Coming to Self

after these years
as iron comes by fire
from the ore
as gold washes clean in the stream
the dross
sifted and sifted
falling away
into the clear water.

At Sixteen

singing a prolonged hymn of expectation
                              it seemed to me
the great force of art would come into my life
like a pregnant wind carrying water from the sea
above the forested mountains to drop its load
upon hitherto unwatered desert

and I would stand
looking up
and open my mouth to drink the first rains.
                              I did not think
the thirst would grow
the more I drank.

The Dreams of Beautiful Women

The dreams of beautiful women
are glimpses of deer in flying snow
moving lightly in some distant figuration
to their own music.
Startled, their wide eyes open
wider & they flee
shuddering.

What is it to have such dreams
to feel in the bone
unearned mastery that transforms?

I dream of wind-fallen apples
still crisp & juicy,
of the sky before snow
gray & stretched
longing for release.

Why Not

a few clear names:
the heart
water
love
        then nothing.
Language is broken
like bread
we eat without
wine
our flesh devoured
with others
in this open room
the table is an O
of silence
and our shadows
do not speak.

Poem to My Grandmother in Her Death

After a dozen years of death
even love wanders off, old faithful
dog tired of lying on stiff marble.

In any case you would not understand
this life, the plain white walls
& the books, a passion lost on you.

I do not know what forced your life
through iron years into a shape of giving—
an apple, squares of chocolate, a hand.

There should have been nothing left
after the mean streets, foaming washtubs,
the wild cries of births at home.

Never mind.   It's crumbling in my hands,
too, what you gave.   I've jumped from ledges
& landed oddly twisted, bleeding internally.

Thus I learn how to remember your injuries—
your sudden heaviness as fine rain fell,
or your silence over the scraped bread board.

Finding myself in the end is finding you
& if you are lost in the folds of your silence
then I find only to lose with you those years

I stupidly flung off me like ragged clothes
when I was ashamed to be the child
of your child.   I scrabble for them now

In dark closets because I am afraid.
I have forgotten so much.   If I could meet you
again perhaps I could rejoin my own flesh

And not lose whatever you called love.
I could understand your silences & speak them
& you would be as present to me as your worn ring.

In the shadows I reach for the bucket of fierce dahlias
you bought without pricing, the coat you shook
free of its snow, the blouse that you ironed.

There's no love so pure it can thrive
without its incarnations.   I would like to know you
once again over your chipped cups brimming with tea.

Dreaming My Grandmother

in a deep green drowning of sleep
suddenly
her torn green gown weighs on me, too!
Pulls down down back over harsh waters. . .
and she runs, singing silently. . .
Scheherezade and the bulbul's song.
O she gave me such a past!
a fan of coarse-matched pieces,
unrisen bread of marriage
hard stubble of man and
—never mind—she said drying her hands:
women are the interior of the world.
Starched curtains winking in a bit of sun:
she had a very small house
but a baroque heart
where desert memories remained in her loving.
O life! she cried harshly young and old
rising
in my dreams   knowing   my grandmother sweeping
her tales of the Russian ballet.
She was ripe with the randy talk of her sex
on Thursday afternoons in the declining light
with pinochle and seltzer to salt her wit.

She had no reason to be happy so laughed
laughed away for life her young girl past
and died   in dream and life a world shattered,
a village among the pines; her broken legacy:
two open hands asking touching flashing
voiceless green eyes that live dream-fostered
as my grandmother waltzes once more,
chews sunflower seeds while her kettles sing,
dips and bows and makes her soups
and plucks a pleasant music from her days.

A Haunting

My mother's hand is fiddling with the spoon
but my face, grown monstrous,
stares back at me from the bowl's tipsy reflection
before it ripples in the clear soup—
shattered!
Ah Madam my hand trembles.
Food spatters on the cloth,
food and the old terrors staining.

My mother's hand is breaking off the flowers.
Petal by petal they die
in the fierce grip of her hands.
My house is littered with dying flowers.
The stink of them fouls the gracious walls.

I dance on the lawn under the sun.
My shadow springs with me
lightly . . .
mine, mine!
My mother's feet are crushing the grass
in my dance.

All of us pregnant with our ghosts.

Child in a Corner

Mama!
Behind your shoulders the world grows bright and pale again.
Yet sit shading your eyes against me grown into a body
strange to me when I am with you as to you.
And the landscape opens out into theatre, backcloths, spectacles:
rolling thunder, artifice, the clutch at the throat!
You!   You squint downward at days you once rolled
like the fleshy apricots between your palms.

The menace in the air means rain.   You snap in two
pencil after pencil rewriting memory.   You withhold
food until certain this darkness between us
can be transformed into a sun marked with your raising.
How lightly you brush the raindrops away!
Your fruit sickens me, I hold the peach with its single
toothmark away from your quick eyes.

Well, I burnt these pictures in your spidered albums—
you'll not catch me!   My palms fit together tightly.
Leaning close I smell your melons shut in closets to ripen
as you ripened me.
                        Where the sun bends across polished pine
floorboards lemon-painted screams bounce into hiding.
They crouch in the swept corners of my lost houses.
Mama!
Make of these snail shells your garbage.
The narrow of that cozy time is mine   hidden
behind hair grown to shield my face.   Your pulling hands itch!
I hated you for making me imagine happiness
out of mute leaves moving through the windows
doubling their dance in the mirror glass upon glass
separated from the barest tip of outside wind.
You did not even give me a board for leaping.
One word only!   Withdrawing to your pillared self
you walked backwards away from my corner, caressing
your iron keys.

I am here
                waiting.   Like the mouse I'll hide!
Now you will never find me.
I rise over you now larger than your souvenirs
or the coffee cups rattling between us
larger than my hatred hard as a peach pit
larger even in my flattened evening shadow
prolonged, elongated, thrown upon your garden
than your head
                backed against the blazing sun.

From These Old Gray Streets

From these old gray streets smelling of salt water,
harbor oil and dirt, I ran for thirty years;
rows of lace curtains rotted in thirty years
of steady breezes over the water.
Poor papa, I'm talking to you—
at my age you had five years to live.
I'm back now for a day, standing on the pier
thinking of you, over that distance.
Wooden houses tumble crazily like abandoned ships
in a storm, and the water nibbles at the pier.
In this bay, your last summer, you tried to teach me,
in this water, where still I cannot swim.

Once Again, the Past

These mornings I wake to the customary room—
grizzled sheet, rumpled clothes, single lamp of sun—
and am puzzled.   Where has it all gone?
The quilt of my childhood has been swept from me
to where?   to where?
Solid shapes I can handle in the dark
dissolve.   My grandmother is shelling peas,
tock tock tock they plop into the bowl.
My mother holds a green sweater in her lap,
a sleeve steadily grows like a snake,
her hands say *click*! the clock grows to suppertime.
How deep the silence around them, like apples!
My father coughs.   The sun goes down
suddenly, stuffed into the cabinet of night.
The drawer slams shut.
And here I am again
collapsed in on myself like a drinking cup
lugged to the seashore for fountain safety.
We've come in strawy sunlight, stunned by salt
glittering under the sun, so many jewels
ripe for the plucking.   But across the barrier beach
the tide's in, the island cut off, waters
lap around my ankles, my knees,
I'm drowning in the present, a wall of waves behind,
deeper waters ahead.

Two

Poems to a Family Album: I

Voices my snapshot cry ten thousand days
of trees the weather of so much life
drying boards of flesh my heart clasped
in children baskets the green leaves
upon my head the fading hands gripped
on calendars hum of lullaby she stood
in aproned age the bone flowering
goodbye my years and now we step
upon the runningboard of dreams in turn
our cry too lost around squealing corners
of one way and piercing silence of margins
and windows beneath old-fashioned eyes
that gaze the dipping cloche
the cottaged lake
the cherry blossom trip
the heaviness of sleep that is your life
and mine a medal pinned upon fulfilling
breasts.

Poems to a Family Album: II

Is there an earth to take when the heart dreams?
Fragmentary, impossible reminder of rented flesh?
It stays, heavy with its bed of grit
& remembers each moment you tossed away
carelessly, a plastic wrapper of your life
sinking as you too into that house next door
to sleep & by the chink of light beneath
drawn curtains must find your way untrammeled.
The soil you breathed will settle free
& you free past dream the heart or soul
no longer worded earthwards the selves
no matter how to come together inch by inch
& grow the wheat of some new body's bread.

Poems to a Family Album: III

How does on down with us the single root
spreading thousand branchward to the runestone
each photograph of jaunty smile, old flivver,
the wedding waltz, baby's dizzy steps;
the years gather in a net of wind
defying all locks.   how make clear
the untamed current of the lives alone
in layering bits—purple snowblossom gloss,
water slipping down the leaf-mashed walk,
star-quilted snow marbled on the tongue
and spring past spring—cut off, a scissors-snap
across the page, so little light preserved
of all the flesh consumed, the grassy hill
asleep on its lie.   each grain of sand
a century tale, and the buzz of this epic
film of silence it is that feeds flowering
the day, sets the feast before blind mouths
that eat too this drum of sound and fatten
as we go to sight before the shutter
draws the smile that speaks the spring before. . .
yes I say my eyes too the shards crumble
imprinted with all the grain of lives
I'd fill—o sweet archaeologist heart!
to dig with toothpicks in augean mold
is your chained task and kindest gift.

A Box of German Blocks: 1939–1969

Was it so long ago he came, my cousin
empty-handed   open-handed   in flight?

And I remember still the voices
shadows thrown against these silent
years between   as if . . .

                       wooden heart, duck heart
                       were you carved on another time?

       There is something which no one really understands,
       A thing too fantastic to weep for,
       That everything in life flows on, passes,
       And that my own self without barriers
       Has come across the years from a small child
       Strangely silent and alien to me.

I hold my own cold hand

Thirty years ago he came to the other world   our world
with a fibre suitcase
a string bag of wooden blocks
his accent
a carved owl from Nuremberg

                     his trembling
                     his shame

Whole villages crossed the ocean in a pocket
I made a province on the parlor floor

                   The magic flowed out from beneath my
                   I saw it all live & move & finally burn
                   & kept the silence

       Each word dangles through the years
       Broken fingers on a broken hand
       Cast against the spot lit wall
       to make a rabbit with two floppy ears!

                   If only I could have murdered those vo

My wooden people gestured in the dark.
The big people   *die ändern*   came to life
in the simmering kitchen light
to speak the same wooden words
unechoing   dead   into a dead time

> I listened to sounds beyond the words
> so slow   so sweet   they came beating
> beating with the systole of pulsing waters
> hushed . . .

I had houses painted with red doors and windows,
fences, sheep, horses, cows, pigs & flowers,
five kinds of jigsawed trees, so cheerful

> and people

and people

> *O jene Jahre!   Der Morgen grünes Licht . . .*

Uprose!   from my mind the puckered lilac
the linen   the blossoming cherry hooped
to scent the surrounding air
A pocket mirror made a lake embraced
by tables crowned with striped umbrellas
Cobbles in the square from pebbles in the yard.

I was a child of eyes

> *Wo aber fülltest, färbtest, reiftest du?*

Ripe as a rowanberry I fell

My cousin came with blood upon his shoes

> See where the green leaves unfurl
> pale umbrellas dusted with ash
> all through the broken grid of shifting
> branches!
> Light patters down palpable to stipple
> face, neck & hands   scarring

What a funny man he turned out to be!
I am ashamed of the way he looks, the way he speaks
those funny clothes   that hat!
Why can't he leave the magic blocks and go away?
... führet kein Pfad ihm zurück.

I want to make another world so small so musical
so dark so soundless so mine
without the deaths & heat—
all I had was this box of German blocks
to make a town against the wilder world.

                    Grossmutter sewing said: we are born
                    to die unknown   and sighed

Yet my hand was larger than the church
my feet could bomb the town to splinters
I alone gave life and closed it
into boxes once again ... such a little
little child!

                    schläfst du gut, Kinder ...
                    It is time for the breaking of toys

The dark was my natural world
light enchanted the mothy others
my herr cousin talking   talking
his nightmares
asprawl on the table in rag doll grace
amid the chipped coffee cups the light shines on

                    ... das heilige Mondlicht Kömmt ...
                    over the voices

The same light rises & disperses
over the smoking chimneys and papas
the coffee voices of my village
that thread my wandering mind to sleep
O weiss nicht wie soll ist ...
                    Kennst du?   The owl cries

24

And in that glass lake the great owl fell.
His shadow cracked against the bedroom wall.
His great wings smashed upon the windowpanes.
Wild his screams break through the impenetrable dark.

Where are the children?
                              The voices

Where should they be in such a night?

                                        Outside the owl.   Inside the voices.

Deep in their beds   screaming asleep

It is the wind   do not cry   it is the wind
see we are here the light is on we are together
it is only night the light we are here
the wind goes

                              hush then hush & hear
                              ... *das Saitenspiel tönt fern aus Gärten* ...

You have broken my world with your giant feet

                              Words cold as cold ashes

Each morning I would hose down my cobbles
hissing water washing away blood
dreams & night for here we are always clean
first & foremost   blossoming snow
on bare branches   water pooling on the floor

                              Die Grossmutter's pastry was rich with butter
                              A little fat never did a person harm
                              said the professor, wiping his mouth
                              with damask

Then why do I cry when I find here & there
a farmer a maiden a shepherd with a broken staff
a painted flower?

> ... *und voll mit wilden Rosen* ...

> You had such a painted voice.

We're Hans and Fritz, O Captain dear!
I sang   making wild noises ...
no desert islands in that *Deutsche* box
no thatched roofs or dusky cannibals
only Brahms blocks and Wolf blocks and
O kömm süsser Todt ...

> You have not died yet
> never as long as with me you keep

So I built again along the Neckar by my bed

> With an owl in a bishop's tower
> they sang to drown his voice but hoot
> broke through the restless air

Come into the garden, Hans, the linden trees are blossoming
Mock orange scents enchant our darkling rooms;
you know the place where bright birds sing?
you know the land where such sweet orange blooms?

> my little dear so *schön*

How we laughed   laughed
laughed at my stories!
they were but stories   *nicht wahr?*
so sweet   so low   so deep   so dark   so grimm

> Like swine, like swine, mutters the
> voice in uniform

Now my turn to go out of my life into another
painted and carved somewhere by someone else . . .

thirty years!   dear Kari woodenhead

the way closed behind   unopened before
to go away far

                        so traurig bin . . .
enough!

                to keep on travelling without mesh bags

my cousin then still lives

                Aber freund!   wir kommen zu spät.

                ✦

Three

Attempts at the Language of Love: 1

I need more than words of bed & sleep
or the language of flesh blankets & quilts of hair,
the syllables that squeeze out of the plump pillows of our legs;
more than table or kitchen words
of the roundness of plums & grapes or the italics of their juice,
more than the conjunction of bread & meat
& the pouring out of soup.
I need words of doors & windows
with their confusion of inside & outside,
of what is mine & what another's,
with their clear, clean geometries that nevertheless
open to so much of palpable sky & light
& change beyond what my eyes control
that it is impossible to forget even for a moment
the tentativeness of my body in space
where it meets in another body more than another body,
more than can be seen, more than grasped
without breaking windows knuckle first & letting in,
with summer, the flies as well.
And more than the moth-chewed language of flowers
crumpled in freeze-dried packets of dictionary slips,
I would learn those words which translate with savor
the speech of walls.

Thank you for your crossroads
where angels roost on sunflowers
chewing & spitting out the seeds.
Each day's noon whistles funnel
across the meadows of your lap
tipping their hats.   And it is all
nothing, nothing but your thought:
thank you.

Thank you for the grass
that waves its hands at horses
pulling the clouds down highways of wind.
I'm gliding straight into your rough countryside
on the strings of your instrument
like telegraph wires of something called love
composed of angels with beards, rustles
in an underbrush of fur, and gray wolves
hunching at the borders, blinking yellow eyes,
hankering for supper.

Attempts at the Language of Love: 3

You were offering yourself in a buffet of stammers—
nubby wind from Canada & its promise of northness,
the platter of crabs between us
on the wooden bench rattling with sand,
lamps dressed in peaked caps of colored paper
glowing against a sun balanced on the engraved line of night—
and I could not look at you turning
red in the sun's fire, turning into red,
into a glass from which I could not drink,
a thing removed from wind & sand
& slowly speaking some disconnected words
in the midst of so much time opening like a tent,
and I was separated from you as I retreated
to the other side of sleep, your eyes open
on the fine detail of erasing beachscape, mine
closing upon the harsh combing of tide you lamblike
brought and wolflike gave.

Attempts at the Language of Love: 4

Scraps.   There's a wind blows back in our face:
the grit of dreams.   Sometimes a warm wind,
memories of May, unthreatening clouds,
the very weightless clouds of dream.
And then the ferocity of the north comes down
on us huddling together.   Rage.   Blue lips.
Fragments of the people we were.
                        We paw the air—
what is this *together*?
When words with wings dive to smother us
they light on crackling shells.
                        Skins slipped free
we come to live on middens, making whole
in rain or wind the bodies we so strangely
piece together.   There it is again, the union of two!
a gathering that, like crossed sticks, makes fire
                        from squibs of wood.

Not heart, old heart—simply hands.　Hands
　　　　like knives on flesh,
old flesh, and eyes to watch the blood
　　　　spurt & stain the air.
Slices of me, slices of you—
　　　　how we are braided!
like a loaf fresh from the work of hands
　　　　& rising.

There are places inside me so secret
not even my dreams have entered them;
so small
not even the moon has found them out.
Take as a gift then
what you have opened to me;
they are no use at all
without you.

The ascending footsteps of morning
do not leave a single tread in the snow
when they pass.
The echoes of the light
linger
in the shadow-prints.

The Heart of This August Day

The heart of this August day is squeezed dry of its sponge of heat.
Night uncurls from distant rivers and mountains, undreaming itse[l]
inserting itself into our damp supper.
We move together across the brief freshness
as animals step to drink at jungle pools
wavering in the pebbly evening shadows
wary and then swiftly yielding
shuddering with pleasure.

Some Old Sweet Novel

Reflections from your window, flowers from your hands—
pieces of the story drift down in the soot.
Beneath my eyelids your particular face.
Your breath in the air when the frost cracks.
Words without shape streaming in the wind
heard only in dreams, caught only when I turn away.
Voices at night telling of wonders, finally:
cold stars spread like ashes in the sky.

In the Steam of the Shower

In the steam of the shower
that conquers the mirrors,
your body drops its outlines
to waver like a breath not taken
between form and memory.

A moment before
this flesh
bound me in love
which now so easily abandons you.

There Is No Going

There is no going
no coming   in you
darkness over the water
parts for your body
where the light lingers

The waiting air dances with salt

Beyond is the boundary of you
and sleep

Dun grasses sing in the clarity
we breathe in and out

Waves enter each moment of sand
then withdraw to themselves
and you fill the night.

Looking at Me   You

Looking at me   you
liven all glances
this moment   cupped in my touch
quickens possession   hand in hand
look!   our fingers uncurl
as morning rims the trees
moving tranquilly   our white plates
shimmer like cloth   opening
the door to a new day
                            delicately
you insert yourself   into my life
its surfaces   now   where I stand
in the brightening kitchen
linking these slow coming-to-day-birth
moments into a life
that swells from within   look!
thick among the unmown grasses
the figs drop fully ripe.

Not Only What You Give I Take

Not only what you give I take
but all I can.
Forget the pretty stories;
I ride at the end of your string
like some whimpering puppy
crying for ease in the drizzled mornings.
And this string whips at me,
twisting into a biting web
spiderly enfolding me fifty feet up
above the dung-blasted grass.
I'm afraid.   No doubt
rocks me of that for all the cradlings
of the treetop nest kite-stringing in the cold wind.
Afraid of what I'll take,
afraid of what I'll get,
going wild, grabbed by the dragging rope.

Nothing That Shall Not Be Asked

Nothing that shall not be asked.
Blue in the room of night.
The shutter claps in the wind.
Black where the echo falls.
The house separates itself from our lives.
Green where our hands have clung.
Across the rope walk of old passion
Red remembered and the sweep of pain.
At the edge of those half-losses
Brown of unmated shoes waiting.
A final evening arrives at the balconies
Silver where the fish cast their spray,
Drop upon drop falling, pooling.
Our days dissolving in the reforming water.

I Never Believed I Would Be Walking

I never believed I would be walking
these wet streets so late, being outside,
looking in upon the tables and the beds
that throw no shadows for me, none at all,
or flower with meaning.   Only rest, sleep.
My life is no longer with the housed ones.
Once all I wanted was all, imagining a weight
lightly balanced on both hands could be carried
not easily but well over the years:
the silence, not the night; the distance, not the cold;
the glowing window squares, not the snapped shade
of a man who looks out at me and is afraid
for his quiet life.   I would take it from him
if I could but in such silent streets
so late there is no need to pretend
or anyone to deceive with sweet lies.

history and my history

Coming to the end of the road
I see another road
an endless fall of stars in the night

say *love*   I wake
sweet christ   the passions
in the dry hotel bedroom
fiery lamps blazing   then frozen streets
I practice the sounds of life
with my bitter tongue of spanish orange
a world of cinders   slow falling of love
your eyes a blue home

Two notes of music we two voiceless ones
an endless checkered tablecloth
of spotted days and.nights
empty soup bowls for joy's fine ashes
brimming with farewells
bells striking another's hours

December of smudged gas lamps beneath orion
peals of alien bells   merry merry
my gift: some few of my words to you
ah you did not understand   my package
flaring with shiny paper   a gift of all
a heap of ashes

In fields outside the heart birds died
remember   and how we loved under
terrible signs   flick of snow
against the knifing rain
within summer with its onward ripening
gathering the world into its orchard hollow
you say *love* not forgetting how
love?

At the final burning:
I was a bronze head in a gallery
you were yesterday's bread
a hyacinth appeared   and lilac branches
a square of sunlight embroidered in blue
your eyes   in the dying fire   once.

Four

Poem of Marriage

In the beginning
we laid the table by an open window
so light could gather on the cups and cloth,
and the bed, so plants stay green
fresh sheets white
darkness wait
melons ripen.

We shaped a world in the fire of the sun
burning silently among green leaves
We loved
when we loved
our bodies shone
shining & glittering with our dance
like fool's bells ringing
time   time   without our knowing.

And then the years passing
wintry light turning ever more finely
more bluely into steel   into needles
into early setting beyond sharp roofs
of houses where other open windows stare
back at your lips   my eyes   joined mouths
at ghosts   old plants and melons
mirrored coldly in cold light   in dry evening.

Steady loss measured by the splendor of those shadowless noons
engraved in the long dusks where summer goes down
to knowledge of fall   time   time   to winter turning
to the unwrinkled night

Night flesh listens in silence to the rustles of growing
rats in the cellar   mice fouling the corners
mushrooms sprouting in the damp
fearful touches
new life
in darkness
growing.

Love-Making

Making love   pairing, repairing   making the circle
opening & joining   making music   holding the instruments
close to warm bodies   (our instruments)   dancing whenever
& however: because   meeting, contacting   engaging, embedding
enclosing, answering   completing, hurting   continuing
in faster rhythm   passion thrust against time   dying
making beds hastily   with clean sheets   reaching & touching
your hand on my arm   passing by & brushing   making whole
hitting the target   unminding   coupling
coming apart   making pots from earth   concentrated effort
sweat & dirty hands   needful fire   making love
making a home   washing dishes   coming & going
sewing lost buttons   damning lost buttons   polishing the furniture
with the grain   finding a poem   somewhere on a page
losing it   finding another   waking with the sun
watching the day   astound once more by coming so intensely
that eyes turn fingers   caressing   sun or rain
entering into fully   receiving   accepting a gradual light
making love   within the sun's arena   feeding the children
splashing milk into bowls   for kids & cats   making a space
for this particular day   smelling the lilacs   aroma of grasses
showering together   drying bodies glistening   with plain water
ungilded, shining   preparing food   salting for flavor
kneading bread   waiting: it rises   & rises again
inhaling the yeast: alive   cracking the crust   buttering hot loaves
eating fresh bread   drinking wine   making love
changing   being: still   planting flowers
turning over damp earth   planting vegetables   weeding & weeding
watering, growing   cursing the work   & the weather
making love   weaving a rug   tending to the pattern
knotting & unknotting   making new   scrubbing & sweeping
making the night warm   & open even without   desiring

ying chess   untalking: then playing   playing!
sing the being   of things   resisting
ging offkey   fitting together   shouting
ning & laughing   because   bending & yielding
eaming   hating the walls   crying
ing asleep at once   making love   transforming
aming   listening to the night   without fear
ning over   turning to   touching
  understanding   then sleeping   together.

To Speak Plainly

not moon but earth   to say
I love   word and act
comes hard for women   in openness
no celebration of breast or flank
only a solid body   you
and inside it   you
bound together in my eyes

to deny a bodiless god safely reflecting
assertive body   bold sex   holding fear
of an unharbored island reef rooted
between a stretched sky bleached
to blue without comfort of shadow
and a sea whose playful curls
are surface lure above the wild turnings
where Poseidon's harsh will rules

to know at last some landfall
in this scrub land where
drunken scents burst from spiky flowers
and fade as we reach them
into the desert's thin pure air

to make the completed dance
you are my husband   but this fierce love
rooted in dry land
drawn toward hidden deeper water
is not only in marriage custom
it is between two
when we are most naked   meeting
across centuries of silence   breaking
into my words   ourselves   as if this love
yes   cuts a refuge in rock.

Under the City: Four Poems

1

Two a.m.   How the wind blows!
Love-making over, we are asleep,
turned from each other in our shuttered room.
The wind tosses us high out of sleep;
waking together   we listen.
The seedling dogwood tree
tomato plants only a promise
the new lilacs and the roses
oppress us with their frailty.
Shall we go down into the dark and the wind?
The house wraps us,
children asleep stir and sleep again
silent in the heart of the night's storm.
Rain crashes down through the windows.
We turn to each other.   Look!
We do not go down but stand
at the open window in the night.
Rain wets us and the room behind us.
So be it.   The storm is beautiful!
In the morning, sun will light the damage;
now, in the night, in the storm
there is nothing to recall us to ourselves;
we remember only our love-making
and feel the cool rain blossom on our skins.

2

Beyond the edge of the city
the children's world begins
and we who love these children
wave goodbye to the lights
and go with them:
love calls us to darker places.
The rustle of grass on summer evenings
beneath bare feet, music of screen doors,
cats and dogs, stirring caged birds—
a world of instinctive things—
gentle hiss of water as night comes down
and our *halloos* after exploring children.
Remembering the old stories of twilight ghosts
we cry out the children's names
across invisible lawns
and will not think of other longings.
With the sudden night in they rush
living in this world like animals,
welcoming the dark, the hidden rustlings.
Damp summer silence comes with them
and the last strip of flaming sky.
O my loves
if life could always be like this!

3

How strange I feel in this bedraggled garden
lacking connection between what I am doing
and what I could understand. Dissatisfaction
separates me from the motion of the day.
October.   Yellow leaves, falling world.
I push my daughter high in the swing;
she laughs and demands *more!   more!*
Her hair floats against the blue sky:
yellow flag of her rising.
At the same time I am trying to read—
the returning swing cuts across the page—
Freud's *Civilization and its Discontents.*
"Life as we find it, is too hard for us . . ."
Around us fall the leaves: scarlet dogwood,
elm, oak, drifting into heaps for the bonfire.
Chrysanthemums burn in the Indian air,
vivid asters and zinnias, glory of autumn.

Summer hesitates in its passing, it is warm
and my daughter cries *more!* and will not stop.
Turning the page, I read on and push her;
she rises in her triumph like a queen.
"We are never so defenceless against suffering
as when we love . . ."
There is a wind, premonitory of winter,
snow and cold, the sleep of gardens.
Now it is sun and falling leaves and gold.
Higher she goes, my beautiful child,
caught by this honey hour, parenthesis of winters.

4

Neap tide in September.
No moment swifter
                or more beautiful
than the one glittering
                with an absence
                                of desire.
To sit alone
            surrounded
                                but not possessed
by all we love
                happens: yes
                                occasionally
& after much pain.
Summer is declining.
                    Overhead
                                birds streak
beyond our touching.
                        Irregular ripples of sand & water
leap
      the eye's boundary.
"The small lights drift out with the tide."
                        One moment
                                    then gone.
We are called back
                to what binds us.
                                Love
which fills & overfills
                    the fountain
                                of our being;
confusion & the price of passion!

No image to sustain
                    no words to encompass
only the memory
                    fading like calico
that returns
            with the tide
                        amid countless diversions.

Lullaby: To Sarah

Child, you have not chosen me.
Child, I have not chosen you.
Still, we're caught past will
as close as life and death
which do not weigh the odds
but lie clasped tight, heart to heart.
I listen for your rising breath.

We are borne along from birth,
must swim a little or drown at once.
Swim, my love, swim!
Sleep only a little, sleep then to wake
(but sleeping, sleep well, dream well).
Run fast, my love, and shout and cry . . .
Child, you will die.

Summer Country in the Kitchen

Summer country in the kitchen, firewheels
keep snow at bay, my hand is burned with love
of you & careless misery sizzling parallel
on the charred burner, the childish feeling
in the air akin to the smell of strawberries,
pungent & shy.   There's the bed
of course, there's passion, half-domesticated,
a rusty cat sometimes not in working order.
It stumbles into the kitchen wearing pillowcases,
grabs the energy of the stove & preens itself
like seeded bread, or lettuce shaking its droplets
on the speckled walls.   Meanwhile, the iron
skims over crumpled cloths & moths skitter.
How could I separate the grasses shoving
at the window from the sky beneath which
they grew ungainly, or the wild strawberries
hunched under them to be trampled & crushed?
The word is summer & it means at once high sun,
glassy rain squalls, the insidious slyness of heat
that strips my skin after my clothes,
as well as the steady stepping forward
from the woods of uninvited ripeness presaging
the onslaught of frost-burned cranberry fall.

Staying Home

House, skin, you give me the borders & separations
of the single life, the bark I rub against others,
the decaying form.   Where can I run to fling it?
Polish graves lie far behind; geometric Greece
encloses me still tighter in blazing courtyards
of draped black figures slung with olive baskets
& called women, firm as trees.   The roughened edges
of France scratch odd blue notes on my doors & walls.
There are no roads lit by accented suns
honed sharp enough to stab the vein.
I will open the door here forever—so I think—
already far from where I started.
How could I leave to chase some errant whim,
a nickel in my fist?   In what direction go,
to what dreams?   Walls upon walls parade:
the steep road up the hill to the market
where I lug myself along, a buttoned passport
engraved with forty years of being, greeting
open faces along the route, my bones shoving
flesh against space.   Paris recedes.   Homely sun
rises & falls not like a postcard photograph;
to what place should I go?   Westering
into a self not yet reached or to an East
whose wild waters drown me?   This place
is measured out in shapes my feet know well:
burberry bush, lilac, the broken rose.   Overhead
jets growl past—and shall I go with them
through formless sky safely above the familiar
manic scene, flying from limp roads belted
with the strangle of cars into some baby dream
of travel? End up mirroring my forgotten face
in the tinned frame of a bazaar shop swarming with goods

whose speech closes my ears? Nothing comes of nothing—
gone is gone. The folktale journey winds home again,
the hero older, bringing knowledge like a pack
seaming his shoulders. Lifting the curtains, I
see the stranger bent in half, then fling open windows
of my flesh & meet, on neutral land, the story
all in one of the going, the waiting & the return.
Waking through the webs of time, I greet
the single traveller where I stand.

October at War

Burdened by the frightening brilliance of autumn
these houses wait sleepily for snow.
Gold leaves lie quietly like Buddhas, waiting,
but the month burns in my heart—how it could be
and is, now, a last bright film before the fires pile up ashes.
This is my place.   Quiet lives in the bones of children
born to promise.   To go out of myself is breaking!
Still, in this looking, breathing, there comes a pointing
beyond and up.   A larger place enters unbidden
with its bitter falls: winter, another world
where planes burst through such blazing trees
pulling me against my cry of *no* to dark witness.
This calm yes this calm; it is a shedding tree
on the brink of yielding.   And then?
The bending is accomplished and the breaking;
the other season whose doors are fire where I burn.

May 8–9, 1972: Welcoming the Bombs

There's a knife edge of hysteria saw-toothing the air.
I feel its prickles travelling along my spine
& the hair frizz.   Green, the rain is pouring
green into the mouth of the May night, green buds of rain
crashing through the flowering shrubs, the trees
& rushing grass, green the color of the rain,
red the color of blood running hidden
inside the snakeskin of sodden days.   The trees,
festooned with the raised veins of their arms,
stagger forward past shattered gates, ablaze
with their leaves like puffs of smoke; telegraph
messages travel along the cilia of their limbs.
They march clumsily, ripped roots bleeding sap
on the squashed earth, streaming rain; if trees
could cry, these would be scraping against night
with scaly noises.   They clank together like armadillos
galumphing out of swamps, or plated armor tanks,
remnant of Jurassic rains.   As it is their barks swell
in the rain that falls in the shape of green flak
out of the saurian age into the time of woolly
darkness, of a single deaf Noah.

                                        —May 9–12, 1972

Afterwards

If all the doors of houses up & down the street
were to swing out, the glass panes brittle
in a cold sun, nothing would change.   Stupid
to imagine I could leave as if the opening
of a door were no more than that, the twist
of arm & wrist.   This house contracts
like aging skin, steam hisses from the soup
bubbling on the stove, candles lit for dinner
play amusing shadows on the walls.   No,
it is not easy to pretend, even with candles,
less easy still in daylight, facing the bars,
cups & saucers stacked in marshalled rows,
vegetables tumbled on the board for chopping
& the bedroom door shut.
                                    What's wrong with dreaming?
The walls retract, three sharp sails
pass stiffly by like salutes to an old summer,
the salt air & soft board pier are as real
as they will ever be.   Married is they say
an end.   Not so.   It's never more than start,
what you will, the common whin sprouting
prickly in a thousand springs.   After all this time
if you were to call me, I would go out bareheaded
in the snow, unhappily, and the snow glazing
my hair would be carried with me as I went.

Now You Have Become the Afternoon

Now you have become the afternoon.
Once you were the morning
as you wanted to be, the first;
Adam in the unnamed meadow,
Eve giving birth alone.

It was time, entering the world
with the garden, made the years
advance in their disguise of days.
Others have taken the first place.
It is afternoon and the light in the west.

It is not all over.   Not yet.
Love, like a July afternoon, can linger.
After Esau there was Jacob, the chosen.
After Leah was Rebecca, the well-behaved.
Even in twilight a remnant spark can burn.

Looking Out Through My Eyes

Looking out through my eyes fragmented women crying for light
dream into the thin winter day blue imaginings, unplayed music.
If I could be another. . . !   The razor edge of frost
cuts through the glass into my tamed flesh.   My life
is all inward, taut as a gut string, a doughnut life.
What will I reach out to?   And from where?   Silent room
at my back, tea kettle whistling in another room,
grass white, ground hard, wind from the north
scatters dots of snow into the sky.
Old friends, old life behind me, old self can't be reached.
My children appear, we drink tea, I move among them,
laughing.   Two hands could not hold all I have here;
if I wish for more, who shall I blame?

Madness

too is a disguise.
Some jumpy advertisement flashed
across the thirty-second screen
before the comic star bursts on:
white face, cookie cutter eyes,
purring steam boilers cooking noodles
in the brain.   Combine!   Combine!
We raise a giggle here for plump
adults foamy with needless desire.
Our faults revive the panic twisting
tissue paper air.   The water rises.
The spit of words, words, words
sprayed from a fluff of detergent
bubbling to the ears, a punch card
file unsorted.   One cold hand.
An extra skin for rent & oh the prancing
of the jesses reporting *caught*!
Thin eyes peep through the hawk's wild hood.

I've never tried it on myself,
not in the winters chock full of children
or the worse summers, dangling in the heat
like some Judy too much punched, the screen
untuned, the days, dripping hints of wild-
ness lost and gone.   You'd have to be mad
to live like this friends say, visiting
in the crush.   No.   My disguise is tamer,
molded of more common cloth that muffles
shouts.   Someday I'll try an excursion flight
dressed in my crumpled jeans.   It's that scream
I shrink from, that strange hawk cry, the water
to the roof, the dun rumble of a comic's plea
into silence, slack skin hanging on a rope of brain,
such foreign pleasures to domesticated flesh;
and the uncertain return, waiting alone
at some strange airport in the night.

Looking at My Face

                you see the skin
aging on display, two lines like scimitars
between nose and lip, two unlovely souvenirs
barring the gates.   For a look, what more?
It's quiet in the flesh, and worn.

White statues in the garden, walls
around the courtyard, in the green air
drawn the trees of bone, their branches
clear.   Coffined roots snake for rain.

A death flows through the veins of bone,
slowly carves a canyon in the bark.

"Women Have More Fatty Tissue
Beneath the Skin Than Men"

Fat fills me out.   Litheness was a time ago;
my feet flashed over the streets—
squirrel feet headed towards no winter.
Rickety, lean years without branches,
"neither chick nor child."
The fat's all around me—in each cracked
thought, doorbell chime, boiling pot,
the need, *need*, NEED, the fat clock time;
chicken fat sizzling, oil oozing from a jar,
the baking, frying, broiling, roasting,
five thousand dinners—a slaughter for life—
butter knifed thickly on bread, the milk
of baby mornings spilled before the sun,
margarine lumps silting my hips
plump with layers of children,
buttocks fat under the sexual thrust.
A fat spring riots in my skin, a lush
growth of tulips, the springing grasses
bursting, the bare bones of place
filling with the fat of buttercups
molded on my frame, each bed and chair
adding its pounds.   A mound of bills
greases the pan, paying for yesterday,
for the teeth that bite fat-rimmed chops,
for the house & car, the fat of the earth;
each year pearled with its fat, ringed
like the bark of the tree—and it is love
lights the fire, burns on the fat of my life,
blazes up at the end to consume in the dazzle
of itself all but the beginning bone,
resting thinly among the raked ashes.

Farewell to the Suburbs

My dear friend Maria Vassilyevna,
Victim of revolution, lover of birds, flowers
And French moralists, a lady of subdued passion,
Raised three sons, dreamt of Moscow, white nights
of Petersburg, Odessa acacias,
Smiled a sly smile, sighed among the pots and pans,
Waited.   Planted sunflowers.   Bought a finch.
Painted the picket fence.
Lived a life of high polish in the suburbs,
Accepting exile as an indifferent matter,
Solitary among her great golden chrysanthemums,
Her enclosures of lilac, damp sweet lilac
Creating April before the apple blossoms came.
A garden much shadowed by trees and tall grasses.
"A touch of Russia," she said,
Excusing her laziness with restrained malice;
Wandered among dogwoods, crabapples, mimosa,
Damask roses, honeysuckle and bumblebees,
Drank, tea, naturally, observed nature and man
"In a small way."
Insisted on refuting *humble widow*,
And took care of other people's children.
Dear Maria Vassilyevna!
"Little innocents," she said ironically to mine,
Babies still, upon first meeting,
Urging me out of the house to the city
As she unscrewed jars of baby food,
Covered Chamfort with a kitchen towel.

Gradually, the narcosis of this life overcame me.
The rhythm of milk trucks, power mowers, garbage cans,
School and supermarket, bonfires and snow,
A rain of children; pressure cooker of daily days.

How we long for such a peace!   No transformations,
No war, no revolution, no queues or marches in the streets.
A dream.   And waking, we still grasp it, are in it,
Or it grasps us, and one morning we understand
How we are caught.
                    Opium days!
And know that life is not like this.

It was spring.Bud, leaf and blossom.   New babies,
Sap rising.   "We used to take the double windows down
Sometime in May."   Under her rickety grape arbor
Maria Vassilyevna pours tea.
Steaming samovar, plum tarts, a swing—
"Goodbye, Anton Pavlovitch," she murmurs,
Talks of "one uneventful life—my own,"
Choosing her words with care,
"For there can be no example that does not
                        begin in truth."
Her French taste inclines her to examples
Which diminish the particular, its silent agony.
Girlhood and dreams.   Russian winters
In modest comfort.   Frosty breath, wooden houses
Of Odessa running down to a legendary sea.

She speaks not of history, but of herself,
Purging her language to the bones of precision.
Marriage in Marseilles.   "He was an older man."
Brief Mediterranean days.   "Still golden."
Then the life I see her in, in the midst of suburbs.
No more than that in all this broken half-century?
Rhetorical days intrude; I bow under their black shades;
They will not go; I feel bereft.   She is amused.

"There is a difference between what the eye beholds
   And the mind remembers.   In action, we are commonplace;
   It is memory breeds heroes."   Her copy of Eugenie de Guerin
   Drifts with the swing.

   II
   I have a lover in the city and bring him my banked fires.
   My husband travels.   Maria Vassilyevna knits,
   Drinks tea, tells my children of Koshchei the deathless,
   Plays waltzes with a light hand on our piano.
   I have no time,
   I have no life,
   I do not love my lover
   And my life goes on unterribly
   Overripe with unaccomplished suffering.

   At night the grass is pearly,
   Scent of lilac everywhere,
   Beyond a suburban sky, fenced in by trees,
   The mind is monarch at Versailles.
   Lights go on in houses, and they go off,
   Time passes.   The children at their games
   Grow and are replaced.   My lover is gone.
   Maria Vassilyevna speaks more slowly,
   Closes her book, picks a yellow rose and sighs;
   Laughter in other houses,
   Dark evening, sleep of children,
   Barely moon, but enough—we need so little light!
   I am thirty-five.   She is seventy-six,
   Tells me a bedtime story, prose.
"In the first house there is an alcoholic husband;
"Behind the trimmed ilex, a paralytic;
"Two children there drowned ten years ago;
"The Baptist family has a nun daughter and
                              will not bend the knee;

"Failure in business; aged incontinent mother;
"Adulterer; impotent husband; retarded child;
"A suicide; one haunted by madness; cancer;
"Pederast son; illegitimate daughter;
"Satyriasis—that I know !"

Peaceful the evening.   Stars shine on her voice,
Unmarred by complacency.   "Have some more tea."
Dear Maria Vassilyevna!   Come from Moscow, Odessa,
Revolution and Marseilles to "cette petite faubourg,"
Remains outside in the night, rustling among her flowers;
What does she know of an absence of life?
Sleeping houses blessed by night.   I look on them with indifference,
What is terrible is precisely that all is unterrible,
Leaves no resonance on the honey air.
Somewhere, somewhere . . .
No terror, no hidden hauntings,
Children like Alice;
Novels where life that goes on so terribly
Springs before us like desire's antelope,
No suburb but the unarmored heart.
Maria Vassilyevna, exile, widow,
Walks among her flowers in the dark,
Picks white-netted berries for tomorrow's jams.
Then sleeps.   She has left the suburbs.
Among the roses a discarded mildewed novel—
Turgenev; her straw hat; her gardening shears.
My life's my own, my hands are full of it.
Tomorrow, if only—*hush*, my husband says to soothe,
But I am not a child and wake, then wake again,
Awaiting morning and another day.   I cry out to him
That I must leave this place and all others like it,
The spirit flown.   And tremble, hearing, far-off
In the silent sky the music of a military band.
We'll live another life!   Farewell to the suburbs;
To Moscow!   To Moscow!   Tomorrow; without delay.

Mothers

Blood bubbles up through cracks in the paving.
Milk flows from broken dreams white into cold beds:
a drift of smothering feathers from snow geese.
Long ago and now: two poles curled on themselves,
holding together a womb creature that does not speak,
pulls   *pulls* at me into the dry years.
Waiting   and   waiting.
Waiting and   waiting.
This is the world I have found myself in!
The world I have found in myself!
Two halves: A walnut, sickle moon, cut melon,
rockers of a chair where the rooted one
sits, watching.   Me.   House-heavy.
                    What am I thinking?
                    What I am seeing.
The old clock ticks inside, circling.
Tick, rocks, roofs, walls, bitter night,
ripe apples, milk pods in uncut fields
where the wild mares gallop with the wind.

The Woman Who Lives Inside the World

1

I am the one who is inside you
kerchiefed
uttering a blessing:
may your eyes feast on arenas of sound
may you breathe like clouds
travelling beyond the sun
May your bones make a latticework
in which I can move outward
into your eyes
into your mouth
into the heart of your life.

2

"I accept the universe."   —Margaret Fuller

At times I turn my back on such raw flesh
close my eyes on the gobbets of fat
break the blood into parables of silence

the world continues:
                     or does it wait
upon my wink?

The sun enters its sky cupola
remember me.

3

I am growing into your husk
like wheat grains under a careless sun
Your skin will plump & stretch with the filling of me
you will thin & grow transparent
I will see the sky through your blessing of skin
Your sheath will split like the bodies of the drowned

Fragments of the new will flicker upon the air.

4

Break open the loaf of yourself
I am waiting where there is no eating or drinking.

5

What!   Run from the bits of flying paper,
the grit?   Flee from the embattled pavements
the whittled crowds?   Slip into the pine trees
somewhere away?   Snakes, my friends, come to greet me
Their soundless music trembles the earth

The insides of mountains are hollow
They wait for me to slip into them
The dark cones scatter their needles
on the cold streets.

6

Where I crouch there is massive quiet
Covered by silence the lithe jaguar tautens:
leaps into the broken air.

7

Something keeps me from screaming
down the long straight roads
unrolling behind me
Your hand thrust between my teeth perhaps
or a memory of kinder times:
rainfalls of sleep
a time of the dropping of masks
The scream floats inside me
I am inside you
The scream rides with us across the corners of the world.

8

I am still making my body in the dark
The vixen loans me her stinking pelt
When I pull it up my head grows a muzzle
my sharp nose inhales the world
At the end of my paws
pointed nails
sever the sky.

9

Maggots dance inside the sheep's head
They sculpt the eye bulging from its socket
The bones stand forth

The rib bones of the world crack open
Springing from the spreading arc
Aphrodite rises
shaking off milk & blood
Her feet trample the maggots
The bones dance.

10

Turn your head
Look down
I am holding a scarlet thread out to you
Come in.

Five

The Great Mother: a cycle
to Catherine de Vinck

Poem of Passage

The child that has come forth into life:
how shall I call him back again?   He is no longer mine.
I have given him his death that he will not grasp,
his eyes that open to all he will not see,
and then it is I
                    I!
                        to whom he calls:
creature of milk & blood who stops her ears.
What is he to me, this rag of flesh crying
for what I cannot give him?
                                His knife
shall shred me finely, his bitterness cut out my heart,
and all his walking into life & death be backward,
eyes fixed on the figure he has made, a monument
of breasts to eat him with, I who have fed him
with the hidden springs of my own breath.
Ah, there is no peace!   I knew it first
yet gave him a taste for the sliver of life
I warmed in my body's spaces—
for this there is no forgiveness.   In my hand
rests the power of the tides, the lulling waters,
the rocking waves, the first oceans pearled with spume;
when I squat over the deserts I gush forth rivers
& he flees ahead of me, afraid to drown.

Poem of Silver

Hidden by the immaculate cold of winter
we are two together, the only world,
heart beat to heart, your paw the shrunken
match of mine but fresher, no bird wing
could touch your skin for soft.   Your need
is all for me, your worship pure of wish,
you are your desire without thought,
and I the silver queen at whose feet
in you all creatures lay.

Poem of Ceres

Sweet my heart the waters fall like silk,
I'll go my love and cast you off to drift,
the puckered waters smocking at your feet.
You stand bemused, your hands fluttering
away from the trunk your baby shapes in light,
open to return my song of gift of sleep.
Sweet my love I offer you my flesh:
the tasseled corn stalks ripening on the bank,
golden ears of corn my heart you eat
and drowse in darkness through the winter's bite.
My cries are ripped from me like bloody birth
as once you were, my child twinned in my bone;
I cannot touch in this long day of barren earth
the one I fledged who drowns into her love
as strange to me as her own fathering;
it was so long ago.   My body feels the pain
of its own vacancy.   If only I could nestle
in your breast my sweet, that place the king
chews on as his own, I'd sleep and dream
and wake and know it to be so, that spring
will heal the jagged tear of your farewell
and bring to me the grace of your return.

Poem of the Sun

And there is the wooden window frame square in the wall,
the panes scrubbed clean, the sun flashing through uncaught
to light the plain wood table where I sit, hands slack.
Another morning & I wait for you to come & make me what I am
the one to whom you bring office and the shield of self.·
For you the wild plums hang upon the thicket trees,
the ripe figs seed the bowl, for you the lamb roasts
upon the spit, the soup bubbles in the pot, the small fire
is reborn, the crisp fat crackles, steam simmers in the air,
peaches bloom into flesh, the dough rises its noon, for you
the feast, the magic charm, the spell spun, the laundered cloth,
the polished floor, the glass as sheer as air, the sun
brought home to warm the walls soon to enclose us side by side.
Without you I am emptiness itself, the ark without its scroll,
the dry well crazed for rain.   Come back in hunger
and be fed, I'll gate you in my fold among the swelling hills
and bind you in the thatch of my knotted hair.
The mother's cloak unfastens for her child, it is the smaller,
glowing sun preserved as guide through all the sky of time
until the window square reflects the moon's last fruit & we go
by its sterile light together into the pure and icy night.

Poem of Two

My mother talked of breakfast or laundry
in language suited to the time and place,
rationing depths & heights so they would
last for a long life.   She planned gray hairs
& grandchildren.   Engraved with age, she
waited mine with me, and *how* I asked
was it with you so long ago?   She stirred
the jam, she did not know how to sit still,
she said it of herself, always pushing
away at what would overwhelm her, chaos,
dirt, and the unfulfilled.   "His roots
tore into the earth of my flesh," she said,
"he sprouted, splitting my shell, I cracked
with the giving of him.   And then I was nothing,
the kettle on the fire; from this
he dipped the food of life."
When had she ever before been given
such language of the untapped mines of self?
You too she said, clattering with the spoon.
I shook my head.   The heavy belly dragged me down,
and the steam hissed in the kitchen like smoke
from the fatted calf slain for the benison
of gods.

Poem of Night

Artifice is the way to look at death.
Gild the figure, mask the face, approach crawling,
incense smoke curling in the fetid air, embrace
darkness, feel the cave damp razoring your skin,
penitent & worshipper.   Isis does not speak her secrets
in your ear, the sow grunting beside you in the dark
shall bear your message beyond the veil.   Her face
is the moon, of all lies the most beautiful
made by man.   When shall it return?   Learn
the secrets of the stars!   If your hands are empty
they will be filled.   The sow's filth is her gift to you.

Poem of One

And yet I can be gentle when alone,
improvising a kinder place for world
than my public self admits.   My knitting
is all sweater, no fate.   The oracle?
To be sure there's smoke and stink
and even fear racing through that cave—
nor is it entirely show.   Death & darkness
are real enough.   Best not forget, flesh
of my flesh, or you will be caught
coatless in autumn's first frost.   The gods,
such as they are, do not send me to warn
of darkness & death, only the lap of my love
mothers me to mother you.   My rusty props
will help you believe quickly what you must.
Then we can play.   It's what I dream of doing,
lying back in the water washing over me,
smiling at stars or sun, bodying what must be lost
& forgetting my uncomfortable role.   Who are you,
coming to me out of season? There's no mother here,
no snake hair, no fat hips slashed by a triangle,
no stillness readying itself to swallow you
whole.   In the sunlight season I dance myself
free to play.   Even Circe sought amusement
in her enchantments, and the gentle pleasures
of beguiling long summer days with more than song.

Dream Poem

Your dream of me is the mountain
you must cross to me
and beyond it the ranges lie
lapping each other in dizzying waves.
Your hunger plays you like a cracked guitar
travelling onward
where the frost nips like crows
& when you reach up to touch me
your hand disappears in the fog.
It's a long way to waking.
If you should look behind
you would find your path
buried in new grass
and linked beds of alpine roses.
The way back is sleep, sleep
to the beginning, before the dream
was bone, and speech squalled
the infant child.
When there are no longer any names for me
drawn from the thousand generations of dream
I will come—no need to take one step—
and give you yourself
piece upon piece.   I have nothing
to do with making you whole.

Dance Poem

I am giving you the dark birds of night—
yes, they are mine, they are mine to give!
I am giving you your dreams unscissored—
not the cloth of remembrance
to fade in the sun, some false idol!
Not only the moon dancing but grass dancing too
back & forth, down & across, over & under,
the dance of weaving & the thread thrown free!
Slow dream dancing of darkness
& animal breath when the tall trees whip
above me & the sleepers sleep.
Bee dancing in a golden stream
through the walls of houses,
through the windows of skins,
through the closed doors of bone,
the papery hive oozing its thick honey
& the swarm swimming on its cape of air.
Ship dancing when the wind comes fourfold
& the ship perched no heavier on the salt rim
than the weight of its following terns sky-sailing
is blown outward on its wind-winged sails
into the clouds that mask the mother moon
and part to give you what you wake not to see.
This is the dark body of the night
that turns its back to your eyes
and waits
and sings
the songs of jars
the song of transformations
and the harsh owl opens to the moon
the song in its throat,
offers a jagged piece of night in talons
if you can reach out your hand to it.

And the slashed mouse dances.
Go
I am singing the˙snake of my own dream
rocking
and singing
I will not harm you
if you bring the flowers
of asphodel
that blow among the light feet
of the dead.

Poem of Return

Do not imagine that I am the lady with the lamp
as I creep whitely down the hallway of night
feeling with fingertips the strange customary wall,
my nightgown fluffed around me, my eyes
cramped with sleep, breeding resentment
to batter my bones.   I do not want to be awake!
But the child is crying and I must reach him
in his bitter dream and bring him back to me.
His imagination raises fears like lianas
fertilized by the spying shapes of night.
I am his earth-made house, the single root.

His bed is empty in a room that echoes cry,
the imprint of his curled form fades on the sheets.
Has he escaped at last from body, fear & me?
Through the open door the full moon stares;
lady with the lamp.   No magic here.   Flimsy snow
& the air is clear.   Snow-spattered he totters
to the gate in his fragile sleeptime self,
unwilling to throw off what he has found,
unwilling to wake & face what waits, staggering
in a drunken trance of arousal.
He'd shake off the pelt of dream,
the unwanted Siamese brother he'd outrun
but it leaps on him & he turns in full-flushed
fear & sinks with ruffled wings into the welcome
I rose to give.   Oh, I'd abandon bed for the award
of such tumbling need!

Sleep.
Sleep, my arms wait to hold you.
All will be well.
The moon is my familiar & blesses the scene.

Child, child:
what dream has so driven you
away from me out into the cold?

Six

Death Poem

What will you have when you finally have me?
Nothing.
Nothing I have not already given
freely each day I spent
not waiting for you
but living
as if the shifting shadows of grapes
and fine-pointed leaves in the shelter
of the arbor would continue to tremble
when my eyes were absent
in memory of my seeing,
or the books fall open where I marked them
when my astonishment overflowed
at a gift come unsummoned, this love
for the open hands of poems,
earth fruit, sun soured grass, the steady
outward lapping stillness of midnight
snowfalls, an arrow of light waking me
on certain mornings with sharp wound
so secret that not even you
will have it when you have me.
You will have my fingers
but not what they touched.   Some gestures
outflowing from a rooted being, the memory
of morning light cast on a bed
where two lay together—
the shining curve of flesh!—
they will forever be out of your reach
whose care is with the husks.

Passing

Nomad moments that fly up like the stray corner
of a shawl in the wind or an encampment splashed
like stars across the dry landscape.   Seasons
when the dawn air whistles, the bells jangle
& horizontal pennants stiffen.   Under horses' hooves
crushed berries stain the children's fingers.
However slowly they move, dreamy charcoal mothers
stepping from slanting tents into the milky day
& the grimacing men who pack themselves like beasts
onto the pathways beyond the hissing fires,
they will be poured away into barren mountains.
Sand the old symbol withers against such lively purpose
& the trumpeted clamor of the life-littered scene.
Sand the old reality swallows them up.   They struggle
in split frames toward invisible tomorrows.
Best not stay to recall with squinting eyes the yeast
of that awarded morning.   What we had is over.
To linger means death; waiting among the boulders
& dry watercourses is folly once the travellers pass.

Life That Has Made of Me

Life that has made of me a vessel for dying
still flies its striped pennants over the heads
of those who walk straight avenues and imagine
for future a matchbox of jewels to be hoarded.
Its hints of endings are no more than right-angled breezes.
It has the balloon's indifference to the clutching hand.
The tea in the teacup is drunk without its knowledge
of china or firing, and it may be so for us—
there is no proof we are not drink for giants.
Only the old habit betrays us—the wrinkled eye
peering over the rim.   In a dry world
there is no place for liquids.   How sloppily the ring
distorts the careful cloth!   Yet not all the maids
hired by masters can sponge these soaking circles.
The pools they make, scooped up in vessels
away from flaccid and illiterate hands,
will become the flagellate culture in which
we multiply and question while we wait.

—October 1973

My Sentence Has Introduced Me

My sentence has introduced me to the language of mutes
who find themselves sprinkled like dull pebbles
across the stony north of their lives.   It's no howling
wilderness, only human gibberish invading the syntax of speech.
I'd strutted my fine language like a hooped costume—
it was the wrong metaphor.   A prayer in the shadows
was needed—no more.   Describing strawberries is incendiary
if gnarled hands cannot pluck them.   *We* is what I practice
saying to convicts and charwomen and all who shuffle
among smoky dreams & wake coughing & wiping their eyes
without even the night smear of hope to dampen the lids.
A word here.   A word there.   I've crossed the border
crouching at the back of a guide with an apple face.
In my new country people with rags stretch out their hands;
anyone is welcome, even those who, like myself, forgot
the country's common speech.   For two words they'll make me
one of them.   Those who know their end lose the sounds of prid

—October 1973

Blood Kept Pouring Out of My Nose

Blood kept pouring out of my nose.
My fingertips puckered and fell asleep
at embarrassing moments and the doctor said,
you have no blood, between the red falls
splashing my face.   My body was tired
of sanity & developed a yen for asylums
where mixed-up pieces could be stuck together
anyhow, ready to flirt with visionary muscles
of beyond-death.   O dreams of symmetry!   Wires
crisscrossed my shoulder blades and clamped
bones energetically to skin, slackened
around my middle and let it be known
that soon the knots would loosen & my flesh
slide apart.   Even when they turned me
upside down & jiggled me around, I dwindled
into a dried flower with bloodless petals
crisp for the plucking, deserted by the blood
that watered a kinder bed.   Six drops of red
on the linoleum is all I get.   So sorry.
Goodbye.   When the pitcher is empty, not even
a nose will fill it up.

—November 1973

Not Like an Open Wound

Not like an open wound, I am an open wound—
a body shattered, no fine iambs or limbs—
there's a place where metaphors come to an end.
                    Drugged, opened to pain,
I resist & imagine that I am the sleeping beauty
bedded behind steel hedges.   Slowly the chosen knight
rides toward me, he will endure what he must,
slashing with his sword at the lovingly curved
armor that is my cradle guard, and kiss me
into waking.
                    Awake, I know
it will not be like this, neither rider nor kiss,
only the slow cessation of that which summoned both
to me, and the folding up of metaphor in the falling
cards of end.

—December 1973

Judith Michele Freedman Murray was born in Brooklyn, was graduated from the New School for Social Research in 1954, and received a master's degree from the University of Connecticut in 1956.

The daughter of Jewish parents, she converted to Catholicism in 1953. She lived in Washington with her husband, James Murray, and their four children, David, Jonathan, Sarah, and Matthew.

Although many of her poems had been published in such magazines as the *Nation* and the *New Republic*, *The Great Mother and Other Poems* is Michele Murray's first book of poetry. She did not live to see it published. She died of cancer, at the age of 40, in March of 1974.